LET'S FIND OUT! RELIGION

BUDDHISM

KATY BRENNAN

Britannica®
Educational Publishing

IN ASSOCIATION WITH

ROSEN
EDUCATIONAL SERVICES

Published in 2019 by Britannica Educational Publishing (a trademark of Encyclopædia Britannica, Inc.) in association with The Rosen Publishing Group, Inc.
29 East 21st Street, New York, NY 10010

Distributed exclusively by Rosen Publishing.
To see additional Britannica Educational Publishing titles, go to rosenpublishing.com.

First Edition

Britannica Educational Publishing
J.E. Luebering: Executive Director, Core Editorial
Mary Rose McCudden: Editor, Britannica Student Encyclopedia

Rosen Publishing
Jacob R. Steinberg: Editor
Nicole Russo-Duca: Series Designer and Book Layout
Cindy Reiman: Photography Manager
Sherri Jackson: Photo Researcher

Library of Congress Cataloging-in-Publication Data

Names: Brennan, Katy, author.
Title: Buddhism / Katy Brennan.
Description: First Edition. | New York : Britannica Educational Publishing, in Association with Rosen Educational Services, 2019. | Series: Let's find out! Religion | Includes bibliographical references and index. | Audience: Grades 1–5.
Identifiers: LCCN 2018011030 | ISBN 9781508106838 (library bound) | ISBN 9781508107149 (pbk.) | ISBN 9781508107255 (6 pack)
Subjects: LCSH: Buddhism—Juvenile literature.
Classification: LCC BQ4032 .B74 2018 | DDC 294.3—dc23
LC record available at https://lccn.loc.gov/2018011030

Manufactured in the United States of America

CONTENTS

What Is Buddhism?

The religion based on the teachings of the Buddha is known as Buddhism. The Buddha was born Siddhartha Gautama in what is now Nepal sometime in the sixth to the fourth century BCE, about 2,500 years ago. He became **enlightened** and found a

Buddhism is based on the teachings of the Buddha, who lived sometime in the sixth to fourth century BCE in Nepal.

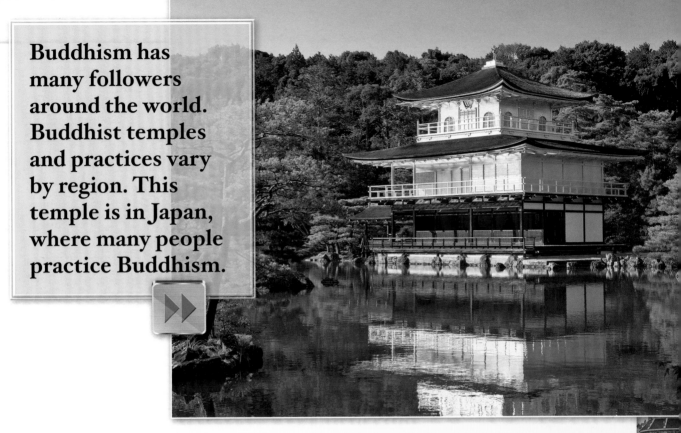

Buddhism has many followers around the world. Buddhist temples and practices vary by region. This temple is in Japan, where many people practice Buddhism.

way to free himself from the cycle of desire and suffering that all living beings experience. The Buddha taught his followers how to achieve this, too.

Buddhism began in India and spread to central and southeastern Asia, China, Korea, and Japan. Today, Buddhism is the fourth-largest religion in the world, with about five hundred million followers. Followers of Buddhism are called Buddhists.

BELIEFS

There is no single sacred book of Buddhism, but all Buddhists share beliefs based on the teachings of the Buddha. The Buddha's teachings are called the Four Noble Truths. The first truth is that life is made up of pain and suffering: all living things experience sickness, old age, and death. The second truth is that this suffering is caused by a person's selfish desires, or wants. The third truth is that people can be free of these desires. The fourth truth is that the way to overcome

Buddhists believe that by following the Buddha's teachings they can overcome pain and suffering just like the Buddha was able to do.

This painting represents the Buddhist idea of samsara, or the cycle of life, death, and rebirth.

pain and suffering is through the Eightfold Path.

Buddhists believe in the idea of reincarnation, or rebirth. This cycle of birth, death, and rebirth is called samsara.

THINK ABOUT IT

Can you think of a time when you got something you wanted, but you felt unhappy anyway? Why do you think you felt unhappy?

According to Buddhism, the goal of life is to escape from this cycle—to stop being born as an individual with selfish desires. Escape from the cycle of birth, death, and rebirth is called nirvana. In Buddhism, the way to achieve nirvana is by following the Eightfold Path.

Buddhism has three main parts. These parts are called the Triratna, or "the three jewels." The first jewel is the Buddha, or the teacher. The second jewel is the

The W-like symbol in this carving represents the Triratna, or the three jewels.

dharma, or the teachings. The third jewel is the sangha, or the community of believers. Buddhist followers believe that the three jewels protect them in the world. This is expressed in a Buddhist prayer, "I take refuge in the Buddha. I take refuge in the dharma. I take refuge in the sangha."

THINK ABOUT IT

Why do you think Buddhists use the word "jewel" to refer to their beliefs?

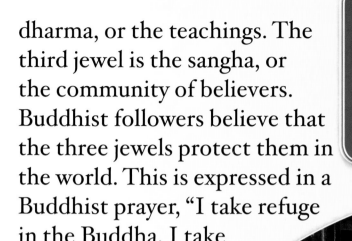

Buddhists believe that the Buddha, his teachings, and their fellow community of Buddhists protect and guide them in the world.

PRACTICES

All Buddhists must follow the Eightfold Path. It teaches that people should not have too much luxury and pleasure in their lives, but they should also not go without all comforts. Instead, people should follow a middle, or balanced, course in their lives. For this reason, the Eightfold Path is also called the Middle Way.

The first step in the Eightfold Path is Right Knowledge, and knowledge of the Four Noble Truths is part of this. The second step is Right **Aspiration**, a

VOCABULARY
An **aspiration** is a strong desire to achieve something high or great.

A wheel with eight spokes is the symbol for the Eightfold Path. It is often shown on the Buddha's feet.

person's commitment to following the Eightfold Path. The third step is Right Speech, which involves speaking kindly and meaning what you say. The fourth step is Right Behavior, which includes laws that forbid bad behavior such as killing, stealing, and lying.

Buddhist teachings encourage kind and respectful behavior.

The fifth step is Right Livelihood. This step involves choosing a job that supports life and goodness, rather than making a lot of money. Right Effort is the sixth step. It involves stopping one's selfish wants. The seventh step is Right Mindfulness, or being aware of one's thoughts. Right Concentration is the final goal of the Eightfold Path—to

COMPARE AND CONTRAST

How is meditation different from prayer? How are the two similar?

Right Mindfulness and Right Concentration are the two final steps on the Eightfold Path. The Buddha is often shown in a state of meditation.

Meditation is an important Buddhist practice. The goal of meditation is to calm the mind and to reach a state of nirvana.

be in a state of nirvana. Not everyone can reach the goal of nirvana, but every practicing Buddhist is at least on the Path toward enlightenment.

One of the most important Buddhist practices is meditation. Meditation is a way to make one's mind calm and peaceful by focusing on one's breathing and sitting quietly and still. In Buddhism, the final goal of meditation is to achieve nirvana.

THE BUDDHA'S LIFE

Little is known about Siddhartha Gautama's life, though there are many stories. He was said to have been a prince in a noble family. He grew up in a palace, away from aging, sickness, or death.

At age twenty-nine, Gautama left the palace for the first time. Outside the

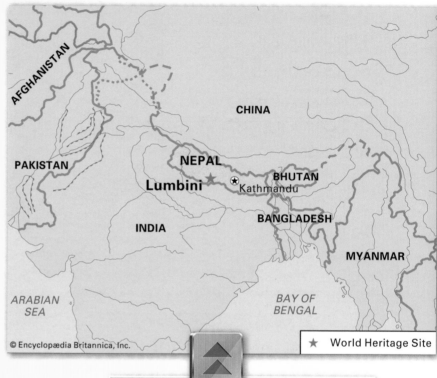

© Encyclopædia Britannica, Inc.

★ World Heritage Site

The Buddha was born a prince in a noble family in Lumbini, Nepal. Many Buddhists visit the site where the Buddha is believed to have been born.

There are many temples and monuments in Lumbini, the Buddha's birthplace.

palace, he saw a bent old man. This greatly troubled him. His chariot-driver, Channa, explained that the man was old and that all people grow old. On another day, Gautama saw a sick man. Later he saw a dead body. Channa explained that all people experience sickness and death. Finally, Gautama saw a monk, who looked peaceful. Gautama decided to give up his wealth and become a monk. He wanted to learn how the monk could be so peaceful when he was surrounded by suffering.

Gautama left home in search of the truth. One day, while he was sitting and meditating under a tree, he became enlightened—free from desire and suffering. In this way, he became the Buddha, which means, "enlightened one." Soon after his enlightenment, the Buddha began sharing what he learned. He attracted followers, who became the first Buddhist order, or sangha. The Buddha sent them out into the world to spread his message. The Buddha himself set out traveling, converting many people on the way.

The Buddha did not write down his teachings. He preached in Pali, which was the

The tree under which Siddhartha Gautama sat is known as the Bo tree, or the Bodhi ("Enlightenment") tree. Legend has it Gautama meditated under the tree for forty-nine days.

This monument in Kasia, India, is called a stupa. It is said to contain remains of the Buddha.

language of the common people. His followers shared his teachings with other people by word of mouth. These teachings were not put in writing until many years after the Buddha's death. He is said to have died at age eighty, in a city called Kusinara (now Kasia, India).

COMPARE AND CONTRAST

Think of other religious leaders you know about, like Jesus or Muhammad. How are they similar to the Buddha? How are they different?

THE SPREAD OF BUDDHISM

After the Buddha's death, the monks in the Buddha's sangha helped spread Buddhism throughout northern India. In the 200s BCE King Ashoka, an important ruler of an empire that covered most of South Asia, became Buddhist. He built many Buddhist monuments and monasteries. Because of King Ashoka, Buddhism spread throughout all of India.

> **VOCABULARY**
> **Monasteries** are buildings that house communities of monks.

King Ashoka helped spread Buddhism throughout India.

18

Beginning in the second century CE, trade bought Indian people and ideas into China. Buddhist monks traveled with the traders and spread Buddhism to China. Buddhism became the most popular religion in China in the fourth and fifth centuries. Buddhism spread to Korea in the fourth century and to Japan in the sixth century. It continued to spread around the world after that.

This historic Buddhist monastery is in Tibet. Tibetan Buddhism is one branch of Buddhism.

DIVISIONS

Many years after the Buddha's death, two major groups appeared among his followers. Today, within the two major branches of Buddhism, there are many smaller schools of Buddhism throughout Asia. These schools have different writings and languages and have grown up in different cultures.

One of the two major groups is known as Theravada, meaning "Way of the Elders." It is the older and more conservative branch of Buddhism. Many people in Sri Lanka, Myanmar, Thailand, Laos, and Cambodia belong

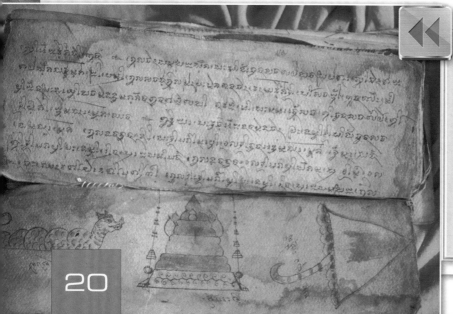

The Pali Canon is a collection of the oldest Buddhist writings. It is also called Tipitaka, or "Triple Basket" in Pali.

Zen Buddhism comes from Mahayana Buddhism. Zen is popular in China, Korea, Vietnam, and Japan.

to this group. The Theravada Buddhists concentrate on freeing themselves through improving their own lives.

The other major group is called Mahayana. Mahayana Buddhism is popular in Mongolia, China, Japan, Korea, Vietnam, and Nepal. Mahayana Buddhists believe they can achieve enlightenment through a life of good work for others. Once they are enlightened they can help others to do the same.

THINK ABOUT IT

Most of the world's religions have different branches or schools of thought. Why do you think this is?

PLACES OF WORSHIP

Buddhists worship at a temple or in their own homes. Buddhist temples look different depending on where they are in the world, but all Buddhist temples have an image or a statue of the Buddha. Worshippers may sit on the floor and chant prayers or listen to monks chant. At home, Buddhists worship in front of a shrine. A Buddhist shrine has a statue or picture of the Buddha. Buddhists may bring offerings of fruit or flowers and place them on

A Buddhist worships at a shrine in Myanmar in Southeast Asia, where the religious buildings reflect the unique culture of the region.

22

the shrine. Buddhists light candles and incense while they sit quietly to worship.

Monasteries are places for monks and nuns to live, work, study, and pray. Buddhist monks and nuns use prayer, meditation, and other rituals to stay on the Eightfold Path. In Theravada Buddhism, monks and nuns live away from society in their monasteries. In Mahayana Buddhism, monks and nuns vow to help the larger community to which they belong as part of their Path.

Monks gather in the courtyard of a Buddhist monastery in China.

FESTIVALS AND CELEBRATIONS

Buddhists celebrate many festivals, but these festivals are often celebrated differently by Theravada and Mahayana Buddhists. The three major events of the Buddha's life—his birth, enlightenment, and death—are commemorated by every Buddhist, but not always on the same day.

Theravada Buddhists celebrate the Buddha's life events together on Vesak, which is also called Wesak, Buddha Purnima, Buddha Jayanti, or Vaishaka Purnima. Vesak occurs on a full moon, usually in April.

The Buddhist holiday of Vesak is celebrated differently in different places. In Singapore, it involves fireworks and parades.

Buddhist monks in Cambodia parade in a celebration of the Buddha's birth, enlightenment, and death.

Theravada Buddhists also celebrate four days every month as *uposatha* days. These special days are the new moon (when the moon is dark in the night sky), the full moon, and the eighth day after each new and full moon. Theravada Buddhists gather to hear sermons, recite **sutras**, make offerings, and meditate on uposatha days.

VOCABULARY

Sutras are texts of the Buddha's teachings.

Theravada Buddhists also practice *vassa*, a three-month retreat during the rainy season, from July to October. During vassa, a person lives like a monk for a short time. A big celebration takes place at the end of vassa.

Mahayana Buddhists celebrate the life events of the Buddha on three separate days. They remember the Buddha's birth on April 8. In Japan, the celebration of the Buddha's birth is part of a flower festival known as Hanamatsuri.

Japanese Buddhists celebrate the Buddha's birth in a festival called Hanamatsuri. During a ceremony, tea is poured on a statue of the Buddha.

> During the All Souls Festival, people put out fruit or flowers as an offering to the Buddha and remember their ancestors who have died.

Mahayana Buddhists remember the Buddha's enlightenment on December 8 and his death on February 15.

Buddhists also celebrate New Year's and harvest festivals according to local customs and traditions. In China and Japan, Buddhists have an All Souls Festival. This is to remember the dead and to bring them peace.

THINK ABOUT IT

Most cultures and religions have celebrations for the New Year. Why do you think this is?

BUDDHISM TODAY

Starting in the nineteenth century, many Western thinkers embraced Buddhism. Buddhist principles of generosity, kindness, and wisdom appeal to many Westerners who adopted the religion. Also in the nineteenth century, Asian immigrants brought Buddhism to the United States. Today, many Buddhist communities exist throughout the United States. Much

Buddhism has a large following in the West, as demonstrated by these practitioners meditating in a temple in Baton Rouge, Louisiana.

as it changed to fit new cultures in the past, Buddhism adapts to fit American culture. There are more than three million Buddhists in North America today.

Buddhism is a thriving religion, with its center in Asia. Perhaps the most famous Buddhist in the world is the Dalai Lama, a Tibetan Buddhist leader. He travels around the world to help spread peace and to share the Buddha's teachings.

The fourteenth Dalai Lama is the spiritual leader of Tibetan Buddhism. He travels and speaks publicly to promote peace and the Buddha's teachings.

THINK ABOUT IT

Why do you think Buddhism interests people throughout the world?

GLOSSARY

chariot A wheeled vehicle for passengers that is pulled by horses.

commemorate To mark by a ceremony.

conservative Holding on to older, more traditional ideas.

convert To cause someone to adopt a new religion.

cycle Something that repeats.

desire A strong wish.

empire A major political power with control over a large area.

generosity The quality of giving unselfishly.

incense Something that is burnt to make a pleasant smell in the air.

luxury Great ease or comfort; rich surroundings.

monument An important structure that is built as a memorial.

noble Having a high rank in society or having qualities of a high moral character.

order A group of people who share religious beliefs.

preach To speak about religious ideas to a group of people.

refuge Shelter or protection from harm.

sacred Holy; something important to a particular religion.

suffering The feeling of pain.

wisdom Knowledge.

For More Information

Books

Gagne, Tammy. *Buddha* (Junior Biography from Ancient Civilizations). Hallandale, FL: Mitchell Lane Publishers, 2018.

Hanson-Harding, Brian. *Ancient Chinese Religion and Beliefs* (Spotlight on the Rise and Fall of Ancient Civilizations). New York, NY: Rosen Publishing, 2017.

Henneberg, Susan. *The Religion and Beliefs of Ancient India* (Spotlight on the Rise and Fall of Ancient Civilizations). New York, NY: Rosen Publishing, 2017.

Marsico, Katie. *Buddhism* (Global Citizens: World Religions). Ann Arbor, MI: Cherry Lake Publishing, 2017.

Nagle, Jeanne. *The 14th Dalai Lama: Spiritual Leader of Tibet* (Spotlight on Civic Courage). New York, NY: Rosen Publishing, 2018.

Thomas, Mark. *Buddhism* (Major World Religions). Philadelphia, PA: Mason Crest Publishers, 2018.

Websites

BBC
http://www.bbc.com/schools/religion/buddhism

Kiddle
https://kids.kiddle.co/Buddhism

United Religions Initiative
https://www.uri.org/kids/world-religions/buddhist-beliefs

INDEX